A MOTHER'S WISH

Author
W.D. Lax

Illustrated by
Juan Hernanez Jr.

Hardcover
ISBN-13: 978-1-62676-733-1 *Use this number in your publication*
ISBN-10: 1-62676-733-5 *For reference only*

Paperback
ISBN-13: 978-1-62676-737-9 *Use this number in your publication*
ISBN-10: 1-62676-737-8 *For reference only*

Ebook
ISBN-13: 978-1-62676-736-2 *Use this number in your publication*
ISBN-10: 1-62676-736-X *For reference only*

Library of Congress Control Number: 2018962084

To all mothers who wish the very best for their children.

Thank You Lord for the vision, the inspiration from family, especially Romond, Treci, Jonathan, and Naomi, and the desire to write.

To my son Jonathan: You are the reason I wrote this book, the words came directly from my heart to reach yours.

Remember, Philippians 4:13. Always. Mamma loves.

Dedication

Doris Dunkins-Mamma, thank you for your pure unconditional love.
Susan Dunkins-Thank you for displaying enduring love.
Alice Hayes & Mamie Dunkins-Thank you for setting the foundation.
Doris and Michelle Dunkins-Through your lives I am reminded that a writer's voice should never be silenced.

A mother's heart filled with joy the day she holds her baby boy. She looks into his dreamy eyes, praises God, and starts to cry.

So blessed she feels to see God's love and His greatness from above, she gives her son a tiny kiss and reveals to him a special wish.

I wish you to grow big and strong and honor God your whole life long.

I wish kindness in the people you meet and in return that you be sweet.

I wish you love every day and that your love in return brightens our way.

I wish you peace and comfort in the time of storm
and that God will keep you from all harm.

I wish you joy, hope, and faith too because these
are the things that will help carry you through.

You, my son, stand on the shoulders of men, who may stumble and falter, but seek to rise again.

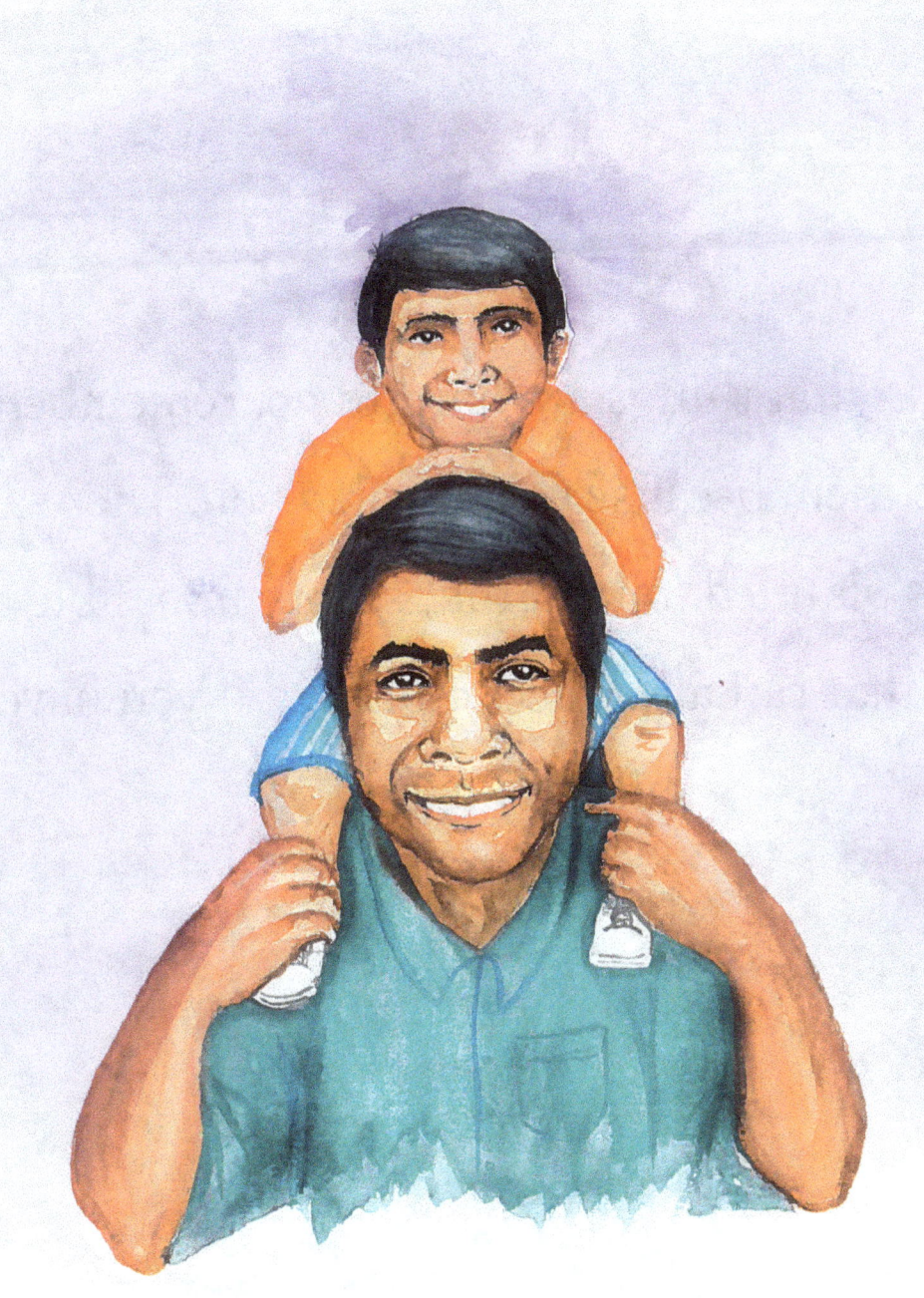

If you find that things are hard to do, remember you can do them because God created you. There are things planned for you that seem impossible to achieve, that can all be accomplished if you have the faith to believe.

"I can do all things through Christ, Who gives me strength."

Philippians 4:13

www.ingramcontent.com/pod-product-compliance
Lightning Source LLC
Chambersburg PA
CBHW081505070526
44586CB00019B/2483